SPACEWATCH

THE Sun
OUR VERY OWN STAR

by Jeanne Bendick

Illustrated by Mike Roffe

EAGLE BOOKS
LIMITED

Published by Eagle Books Limited, Vigilant House, 120 Wilton Road,
London SW1V 1JZ, England

Text © 1991 Jeanne Bendick
Illustrations © 1991 Eagle Books Limited

A CIP catalogue record for this book is available from the British Library.

ISBN 1-85511-078-4

Printed and bound at Worzalla, USA

Contents

The Sun

What lights the day?
What heats the Earth?
What makes plants grow?

4

What keeps the planets in their
 places?
It's a certain star.
It's the Sun.

Did you know that the Sun is a star?

Our Sun isn't all that special in the universe. It's an ordinary, middle-sized yellow star. There are 100 thousand million other stars like it in our neighbourhood in space, the **Milky Way Galaxy.**

We are here

But no other star in the universe is as important to us.

Where the Sun shines on Earth, it is daytime. It is night on the part of the Earth where the Sun isn't shining.

Where the Sun shines for many hours of the day, it is summer on Earth. Where the Sun shines for fewer hours, it is winter.

The Sun's energy keeps every living thing on Earth alive.

The Sun's energy lifts water out of the oceans and makes rain.

The Sun's energy makes hurricanes. But it also makes rainbows.

The pull of the Sun's gravity keeps the planets from leaving their orbits and flying off into space. An **orbit** is the special path that a planet follows around the Sun. **Gravity** is a force that pulls things towards each other.

Gravity keeps everything in the solar system together. The **solar system** is the Sun and all its planets.

If the Milky Way is our neighbourhood in space, then the solar system is the street in which we live.

What is the Sun like?

The Sun may be just an average star in the universe, but in the solar system it is a giant. More than a hundred Earths could fit, side by side, across the Sun.

The Sun is a huge, bubbling, flaming ball of gas. It is hotter than the hottest thing you can imagine. Deep inside the Sun the temperature is millions of degrees hot. On Earth, 30 degrees Centigrade (C) is a very hot day.

Hydrogen is the fuel that keeps the Sun burning. Hydrogen is a gas. Inside the Sun, hydrogen is being changed into another gas, **helium.** The Sun is a special kind of giant nuclear power plant.

The Earth's average distance from the Sun is 150 million kilometres. It would take 1,300,000 Earths to make a ball as large as the Sun.

If you could look inside the Sun, you would see that it is not the same all the way through.

In the centre, rather like the stone of a giant peach, you would see the **core.** The core is twice the size of Jupiter, the biggest planet in the solar system. The temperature at the Sun's core is about 15 million degrees C.

Deep inside the Sun, churning, burning bits of matter crash into each other. They knock themselves apart and then come together again in different ways. This changes them from one gas into another as they move out towards the surface. The journey may take millions of years.

The surface of the Sun

The shining surface of the Sun is a sea of boiling gases.

Pinhole

NEVER, NEVER, NEVER LOOK DIRECTLY AT THE SUN – NOT WITH YOUR EYES OR THROUGH BINOCULARS OR A TELESCOPE. IT COULD MAKE YOU BLIND.

Sun image

The Sun has an atmosphere, but it's not like the blanket of air around the Earth. It's made of very hot particles of gas.

We can see the Sun's atmosphere when the Moon covers the Sun completely. This is called a **total eclipse.**

During a total eclipse, the Sun's inner atmosphere looks like a thin, bright ring around the black shadow of the Moon. The Sun's outer atmosphere, which is called the **corona,** extends past the ring in rays, like flower petals.

Corona

Inner atmosphere

But the Moon is much smaller than the Sun! Can you guess how something as small as the Moon can cover something as big as the Sun?

Try this. Hold your hand up in front of your face. Close one eye.

Can your hand cover a car? A tree? Even a house?

But your hand is much smaller than any of those things! Now you know how the Moon can cover the Sun. The Moon is much *closer* to us than the Sun is.

Sun storms and sunspots

Sometimes, giant tongues of flame leap up from the boiling, fiery surface of the Sun. These tongues may loop back into the Sun. Or they may spurt out into space for over 150 thousand kilometres. That's almost half the distance from the Earth to the Moon.

Sometimes, there are huge explosions on the Sun. These send out waves of light, heat, X-rays, and other kinds of **radiation** across space in all directions. Radiation is energy given off by the Sun. It can take many different forms. Each kind of radiation carries a different amount of energy.

Whatever type of radiation it is – heat, light, or any other kind – it takes about eight minutes to travel from the Sun to the Earth.

Here is a close-up picture of the Sun's surface. The Sun looks as if it has freckles. These are called **sunspots.** They come and go on the Sun. Some sunspots are bigger than the Earth.

Sunspots are a special type of electrical storm. They are magnetic. Magnetism, like gravity, is a force. Magnetism and electricity usually go together.

The sunspots' energy reaches all the way to the Earth. It can interfere with radio and television signals. More important, sunspots can affect the weather on Earth.

Sunspots seem to form and then disappear in patterns. For about eleven years, the number of sunspots keep growing. Then, for the next eleven years or so, there are fewer and fewer. Scientists don't yet understand why this happens.

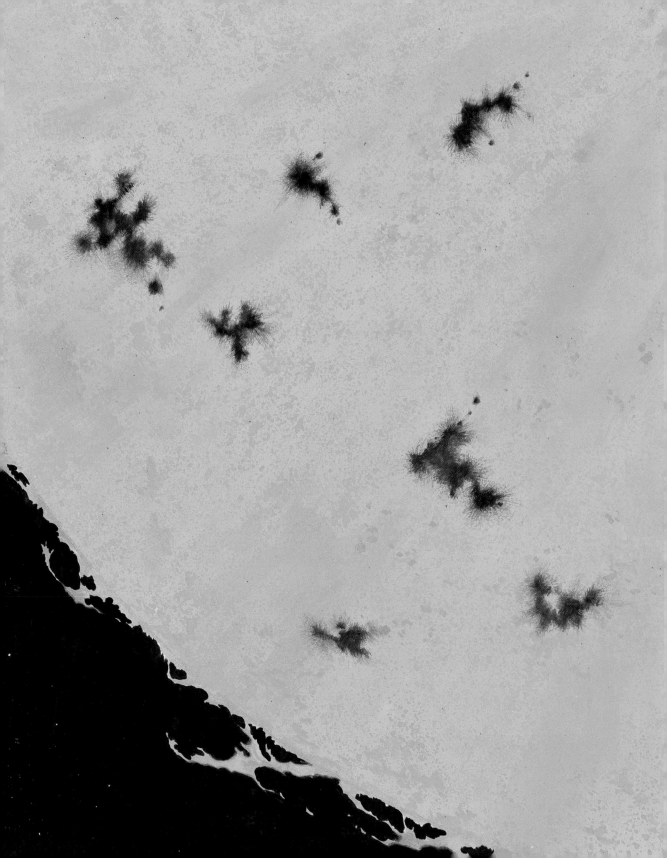

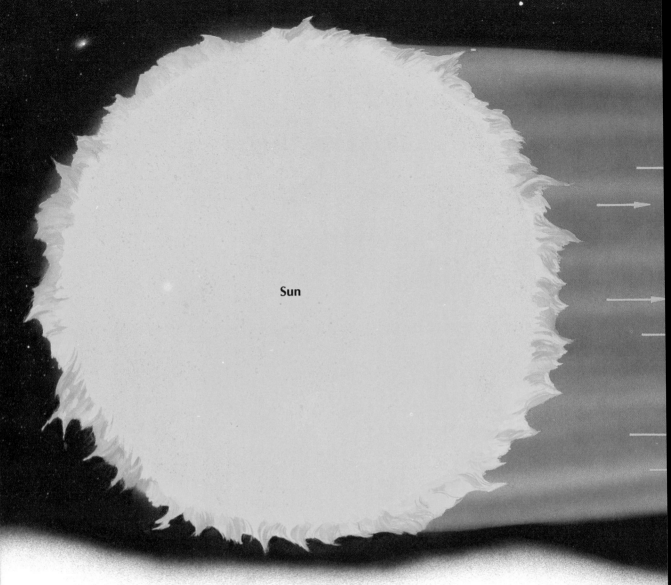

Sun

Wind from the Sun

A solar "wind" blows out from the Sun. You can't feel this wind. It's not like the kind of wind caused by moving air that we have on Earth. It's like a rushing river of electrically charged particles.

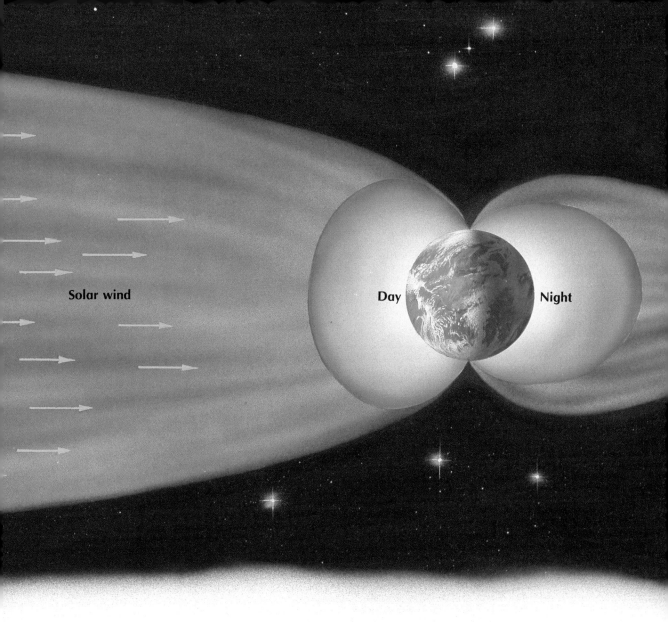

Solar wind

Day

Night

Those particles would be harmful if they reached the Earth, but the magnetic field of the Earth turns them aside.

Did you know that the Earth is a giant magnet? This is what makes a compass needle point north.

How the Sun began

Scientists think that the Sun began as an enormous cloud of gas and dust. Over millions of years, the matter in the cloud came together. The cloud got hotter, denser and rounder. Then, about 4½ thousand million years ago, it got so hot, it began to burn. There is enough fuel in the Sun to keep it burning for about another 5 thousand million years.

Stars are born in clouds of dust and gases, called nebulae.

How the Sun might end

As its fuel is used up, the Sun will swell into a **red giant** star. It will spread throughout the solar system until it almost touches the Earth.

The planets Mercury and Venus will be swallowed up by the growing Sun. They will burn up. Earth, too, will become a cinder.

Then the Sun will cool and shrink until it is a **white dwarf** star. And, at the end, it will be nothing but a burnt-up, dead, **black dwarf** star.

But long before any of those things happen, Earth people will surely have left our planet to live on other planets around other stars.

Index